Stock Options

Day Trading Strategies

The **12** Intrinsic Rules of Day Trading

© Copyright 2015 - All rights reserved.

This document is geared towards providing exact and reliable information in regards to the topic and issue covered. The publication is sold with the idea that the publisher is not required to render accounting, officially permitted, or otherwise, qualified services. If advice is necessary, legal or professional, a practiced individual in the profession should be ordered.

From a Declaration of Principles which was accepted and approved equally by a Committee of the American Bar Association and a Committee of Publishers and Associations.

In no way is it legal to reproduce, duplicate, or transmit any part of this document in either electronic means or in printed format. Recording of this publication is strictly prohibited and any storage of this document is not allowed unless with written permission from the publisher. All rights reserved.

The information provided herein is stated to be truthful and consistent, in that any liability, in terms of inattention or otherwise, by any usage or abuse of any policies, processes, or directions contained within is the solitary and utter responsibility of the recipient reader. Under no circumstances will any legal responsibility or blame be held against the publisher for any reparation, damages, or monetary loss due to the information herein, either directly or indirectly.

Respective authors own all copyrights not held by the publisher.

The information herein is offered for informational purposes solely, and is universal as so. The presentation of the information is without contract or any type of guarantee assurance.

Table of Contents

INTRODUCTION

Can you make money in the stock market as a beginner?

This question must have been bothering for you for some time. Everyone knows that stock trading is all about one thing, making money. We must consider, however, that the stock market is also about winning and losing.

In the stock market, it really doesn't matter if you are a professional or a beginner, as long as your investment choices are providing you with modest results. You will survive in the market as long as the "tips" you receive gain you profits. As a beginner, the key to your gain is on how to access the information that will bring you income. Reality is that you will not become a big shot investor instantly. That will come later. For now, you are gaining experience.

This eBook aims to grant you access to the information you need to trade successfully. It further provides you with the full understanding of what day trading is all about, the current market, the risks and pitfalls involved, the choice of software, strategy and techniques that you need to develop if you want to survive and succeed in this business.

CHAPTER 1 – INTRODUCTION TO DAY TRADING

Day Trading is becoming popular on the internet as more people are looking for diverse ways to invest whatever money they have in hopes of gaining more profit. Some use it as a way of earning extra income, while others do it full time. Trading can work for you in either of these categories.

Day Trading is simply taking advantage of shares that frequently change value, all throughout the day. This requires a lot of information, as well as a keen sense of the proper time to buy and sell stocks. You must stay well informed of what is happening in the news and keep tabs on the latest market trends.

With modern technology, gaining access to the needed information is no longer remote and impossible. Active trading involves fast actions and having the most information possible in order to lessen the risks involved in the trade.

Why Do You Have to Invest in Day Trading?

People get into day trading because of its potentially enormous profit. Trading carries a lot of benefits for those who can manage to withstand its inherent pressures. Here are some benefits you can have from the trading activity.

Financial Independence

Most traders are self-employed. In trading, you are answerable to no one and are free to do what you want with your time without worrying that you will not be pleasing others. Since trading is a business, you can reap the full measure of your labor. Given time, you can end up as a successful trader if you pay close attention to details.

Euphoria

Seldom, in other businesses, could you experience the static emotion of euphoria that comes with earning a huge profit through your own efforts like you can with day trading. This benefit easily erases all the stress you have accumulated through your day-to-day activities.

Status

Day traders occupy a certain status in the communities where they live. Traders are known for making their own way and reputed to live by their own rules. There are some people who are easily threatened by others, they aren't likely to be traders.

Understanding How Day Trading Works

Trading stocks means the act of selling and buying stocks. Hence, when 1000 shares of stocks were traded on a single day, it means 1000 shares were bought and sold. It is necessary for a trader who is just beginning to understand the basics of how the market works, in order to trade successfully.

There are two ways through which you can conduct trading. One is through the physical exchange center. Nowadays trading is moving off the floors and onto electronic networks, the second way trading can be conducted. There are traders who oppose this trend. NASDAQ is an example of electronic trading.

Are you familiar with the scene of people shouting while watching monitors and appearing to be extremely out of control while others are entering data? This is a view of what is actually happening inside a stock exchange. A typical example is the New York Stock Exchange (NYSE). This is how trading works on the floor. Activities in NYSE are coursed through licensed brokers, so you can choose your broker and ask him to buy let's say 100 shares of ABC at market.

With your order, the broker's department sends the order to the floor clerk at the exchange center. The clerk alerts the floor traders to find another floor trader who wants to sell 100 shares of ABC. Upon finding the trader who wants to offer his shares in the market, the two traders will then agree on a price before arriving at a complete deal. Your broker will then call you back with the final price. It will take a few minutes or at times, a few hours before a trade can be completed.

We also, have a type of trading than runs through an electronic system. An electronic market integrates its activity within a web interface, providing a greater market for electronic traders and investors. With this type of trading you don't need to travel or go to the NYSE but you can do all of your buying and selling stocks or shares online. There is no human who is directly involved in any stage of trading, making the method fast and efficient. Many companies actually prefer this method of trading as corruption is lesser if not totally out of the scene. Though brokers are still in charge of your business here, as they are the ones who can gain access to exchange networks and use the system to find buyers or sellers, you will find that electronic trades give you almost instant confirmation of trades.

As you begin to understand the market, you are getting closer to understanding investing. Those who are new to this industry must take the time to research every aspect of the market. When something goes wrong, it is important to know what's going on behind the scene.

Along with understanding how trading works, an investor must likewise understand how the market works. There are many factors that affect the movement of stocks in the marketplace and a professional investor understands these factors and is prepared to meet market movements.

Trading, if done wisely can give you a great chance of meeting your investment goal.

Necessary Tools in Successful Day Trading

To gain profit in day trading, you need to have enough capital investment. Experienced traders usually recommend a starting capital of at least $100,000. So if you are a beginner in this trade, either you have enough money in the bank which you are willing to risk, or save until you can gather enough funds to start trading. Here are the tools you need to succeed, other than your equity.

- **Equipment**

    Modern day trading is now accessible via digital software integrated into a package of electronic devices like computers, monitors, routers and modems. Traders are using these facilities to keep abreast of the market on a 24/7 basis and in order to gain access to a Level II trading service which provides real-time quotations of individual market makers.

    For anyone who isn't a NASDAQ member organization or a registered market maker, Level II access is considered the highest level of information that is available. To avoid paying commission to a broker for every trade made, active day traders need to use an electronic communication network (ECN). Memberships to ECNs such as *Instinet, NYSE, and SelectNet* are fee-based and are subject to approval. Traders must regularly monitor real-time news outlets to keep abreast of current market movements, as these can largely affect their market positions. Costs of running all these facilities can run thousands of dollars per month.

Some traders who only occasionally day trade will rely upon online brokerage accounts to provide them with information and implement trades instead of going through Level II or ECNs. However, they pay an additional cost to the broker and get delayed information. Therefore, if you intend to become a successful full-time broker, a minimal cost and immediate access to information can make the difference between a loss or a profitable trade.

- **Substantial Equity**

    If you want to engage in short selling, e.g. selling shares of stocks you don't own in anticipation that the price will lower, you need to use margin accounts. Once you short sell, you are assuming unlimited risk since there is no limitation on how a stock price can move before you can cover the short position. On the other hand, purchasing stock entails limited risk since the stock price can't go below zero.

    A margin account is like a credit line secured by the cash or value of stocks in the account. The broker will provide you loans for funds which are subject to legal provisions in order to acquire or maintain your stock positions.

    The Securities and Exchange Commission (SEC) declared in 2001 that anyone who makes more than 4 trades within a five-day period in a margin account will be called a "pattern day trader". Basically, a typical margin account requires a deposit of $2,000 to open, but NASDAQ and NYSE day traders, are required to keep $24,000 equity in their accounts on any day trading occurred, even if they have not done any short selling. This amount is also the minimum rate for margin trading if you are buying or selling short. A successful trader may recommend you have at least $50,000 to $100,000 in order to have sufficient power to buy or sell stocks in the $100 to $500 price range.

For example you trade 1,000 shares at a time, you can do this with 1-3 stocks since a margin of 25% gives you the buying power of $200,000 to $400,000. However, acquiring a large number of shares is required to make a profit of 1%-3% per trade. When you purchase 1,000 shares of stocks at $20, the total cost would be $20,000 for stock and $7 for commission). Here, you are providing the entire purchase price.

If later in the day, you sell the same stock for $20.75 per share. Your profit would be $20,743 ($20,750 - $7 commission) and your profit is $736 ($20,743 - $20,007. Since you have not borrowed money, you will see that the percentage gain on the total value of the trade and your actual cash invested are the same – 3.6% ($736/$20,007.

If you can repeat the same performance for each of the 252 trading days, then you will be earning 907 percent. By the end of the year, your $20,007 investment will grow to $185,000 in your account. The possibility of a high return, is what makes day trading appealing to most though it is unlikely that these results would occur daily.

Day traders can operate in stocks, options, commodities or currencies since they are placing large significance on the price and not on the value.

Though there may be some variations in each market the principles of day trading apply to all.

1. Opening and closing position are kept daily and no securities overnight
2. Transactions are initiated based on technical analysis
3. To take advantage of projected movement, buying or short selling is a requirement

- **Knowledge**

    Traders never concern themselves with the basic value of the company whose securities they are trading because of the shorter holding period (usually measured in minutes). They are more concerned with the mindset of the market. Mindset refers to the hopes and apprehensions of individual shareholders while they buy and sell.

    Traders usually focus on indicators that signify those emotions, rather than on factors such as price-to-earnings ratios, competition, and market share.

    Rumors and hearsay often affect market movements that traders will watch out for. In short, trade players are giving more significance on "insider's tips" than on actual news.

    Trade investors arrive at a decision based on technical analysis found using computer software and programs. To master this technology, they need to familiarize themselves with individual stock price movements based on previous performances.

    Visual charts are used by traders to analyze price movements and trends such as moving averages and relative strengths. Day traders look for patterns and try to interpret them. Patterns in stock prices, such as head and shoulders, pennants, and flags are being identified and analyzed to project short and medium-term price direction.

Traders don't actually prepare these charts but rely on professional services extended by companies such as *IQ charts, OmniTrader,* and *MotiveWave.*

Successful traders usually base their interpretation on experience and how they relate to the situation.

- **Experience**

    Learning to day trade successfully can take a long time. In order to lessen risks in actual trading, some people start out by "Paper Trading". This is a process that makes imaginary buys and sells using actual market data, though not risking real money. This is purposely for identifying potential opportunities for profit while teaching the mechanics of the marketplace. There are many brokers who will allow you to create a virtual account to facilitate this.

    Paper trading can't prepare you for the psychological pressure created by risking real money. It's like learning to tame a lion by reading several books on how. Being face to face with a real lion is never like seeing one on television or in a movie. Having to recall their first experiences in trading, an experience trader wondered which comes first. Is it losing money or finding success? Others may tell you that there are more easy ways to make your living than trading.

- **Discipline**

    Self control and discipline are a must in trading. There is a very thin line that separates gambling from trading and many traders are more addicted to the act of making money than their reason for trading. Addicts can afford to lose more than what is necessary just to feel the rush of adrenaline as they win once and lose more than 10 times their winnings.

While discipline and self control are important in decision making, it's hard for a trade player to let go of an opportunity to trade even if the signals of his strategy do not dictate a trade. A trader finds it hard to refrain from making a trade unless conditions are right. If you truly want to gain success in trading, you need to develop a set of strict rules that separate your emotion from the business.

Once you have a plan it is critical to stick to that plan for a profitable day of trading. An example of the rules that traders adhere to includes placing a stop-loss order in simultaneously with the execution of a trade to limit any loss to a fixed percentage of investment.

A trader may also close a position when an event did not occur as anticipated. Regardless of profit or loss, he may never keep a position overnight under any circumstances.

- **Commitment**

Trade players spend long hours of preparation before actual trading occurs. They can spend 70-80 hours a week focused intensely on the market during open hours in order to identify short-term opportunities for profit. Usually, a trader spends his nights preparing to participate in the next day's trading sessions. They will also keep their ears open to any news stories that include financial earning reports or market projections, as these can potentially affect their market position. After a lot of preparation, they can finally participate in trading in international markets which are usually open in the United States in the evening.

Basic Rules You Must Learn in Day Trading

There are several rules that you need to master to become successful in day trading. Here are 12 Basic Stock Investing Rules you should know as a beginner.

Rule # 1 - Buy Low-Sell High

This is basic, yet majority of traders appear to do the exact opposite. Your ability to buy low and sell high will determine your success rate in the stock market.

Rule #2 - Stock Market is Always Right and Price is the Only Reality in

Trading

Staying long in the market means doing exactly what the market is doing. This also implies following the direction the market is leading. If you go the opposite direction, then you will end up losing money.

If the stock market is going up and you fall behind, the market is right and you are wrong. If the market is going down and you stay long enough, you are again wrong. Wrong moves in the opposite direction of the market equates to a loss in day trading.

The longer you stay with the market movement; the more money you will earn. The longer you choose to stay wrong with the stock market; the more losses you will incur.

Rule #3 - What goes up in the market will go down and what has gone

down will come up

The market moves in only two, opposite directions, up and down. When a stock or the market is down, there's no way for it to go but up. The same rule applies for the opposite direction. The more extreme the movement of stocks or the market in one direction, the more extreme the movement in the opposite direction will be once the market trend changes. This is known as the ***"Trend always changes Rule."***

Rule #4 – There Are No Clear-Cut Reasons Why Stocks or Markets Make Large Directional moves

In day trading, you are dealing with market perception and not reality. So if you try to look for certain reasons why stocks or market make huge market movements, it will probably take you a long time and probably cause you great losses before you can find it, if ever there is one.

While it is necessary to know that stocks and the market are moving, we can't presume to know why they are moving that direction. This is why trading is based on direction and duration. It's a fact that traders are only concerned with these two factors and not on the "whys". If you think you can afford to waste more time on assessing every reason, then it's always up to you.

One thing is certain in trading, market movement is not rational and there's no sureness as to its movement. A lot of factors get into the way when trying to asses movements based on the certainty of facts.

Rule #5 – Stock Markets Move in Advance of News.

Some people base their trading decisions on news or supportive fundamentals. If you invest in a stock only when it is clear that it is heading in a certain direction, then you may be too late. Others have surely gone ahead of you.

If you want to rake in profits, you need to position yourself ahead of others or before the occurrence of a market directional trend. The market reaction to the news, regardless of its state, in a "bull market", is often positive. The market reaction to the same news in a bear market is often negative.

You need to get positioned before the directional trend takes over the market. The market reaction to good or bad news in a bull market is often positive. The market reaction to the good or bad news in a bear market will be negative more often than not.

Rule #6 - Long Trend Comes with Big Profit

Trend is the basis of all profit in trading investments. To make a big profit, you need to find long-term trends. The secret to success is knowing when to get aboard a trend and stick with it for a longer period to maximize your earnings. Contrary to short-term investment, if you want to catch sizeable profits, get into large market movements.

Rule #7 – Discipline is a Necessary Skill in the Market.

If you want to have a chance of gaining success, then let your profits run and cut your losses quickly. Discipline is not the only skill needed to make money in the markets, but it is a necessary skill. If you do not keep yourself in line, you will not make money over the long term. This is a stock trading "system" in itself.

Rule#8 - The Efficient Market Hypothesis is a Myth.

EMH or Efficient Market Hypothesis is an investment theory that rationalizes the impossibility of beating the market because market efficiency always causes existing share prices to reflect and incorporate all relevant information. EMH further stipulates that stocks always trade at their fair value on stock exchanges, therefore making it impossible for traders to purchase low-value stocks to sell high. In short, this hypothesis says that it is impossible to gain from the overall market through stock selection and market timing and proposes the only way traders can profit is through buying high-risk stocks.

This hypothesis is irrelevant and immaterial as the perfect competition model is not based on anything. Successful traders have simply gotten some good information and act on it as soon as they can.

Combining superior information for some with the usual panic for others as losses accumulated caused by buying high and selling low creates inefficient markets.

Rule # 9 - Traditional Technical and Basic Analyses Are Not Enough to

Gain Profit Consistently

Market timing is relevant to success with the integration of optimization, data mining, subjectivism and other statistical tricks and data manipulation. Without them, you will never have any chance of success, as traditional and fundamental analyses are not enough to give you a jumpstart on the competition.

Rule #10 – Never Trust Other's Ideas and Advice Unless They Are

Successful Traders

Software vendors, market commentators, brokers, and stock trading system sellers will always manipulate your ability to make decisions by giving you unsolicited advice. They usually have their own reasons for doing this. Unless they use their own finances in trading and have traded successfully for years, never solicit advice from them. You must learn to make your own trading decisions based on what you have learned. Most of the time, traders learn the trade the hard way.

Rule #11 – When a Trader Takes a Large Loss on His Position or Portfolio is the Worst Thing That He Can Do

This is a common experience for most traders, especially in their first few years in the business, but timing can help you prevent this. To avoid being in this kind of situation, don't buy stocks when they are high. Buy stocks when they are low and sell when they are high. Your starting point is crucial in determining your total return. So if you buy low, your long term investment result is undeniably better that those traders who bought stocks at high prices.

Rule #12 – For a Successful Trading Method, You Must Not Take More Than 4 - 5 Hours a Week

Longer hours spent trading means more hours of stress. When you are under stress, there is greater possibility that your perception is blocked. If this is the case, your decision-making is hampered and cannot operate fully. For a majority of us, particularly for beginners, 1-2 hours per week is recommended with no stress involved. Limiting the hours you spend in the trade will allow you to manage your stress.

Critical Things You Must Learn About Trading

As you progress into day trading you need to familiarize yourself with NASDAQ and NYSE. These two organizations are stock exchanges. A stock exchange is where people go if they want to trade stocks. These stock exchanges earn through fees they charge when they arrange deals between buyers and sellers. A company that wants to publicly trade its shares of stocks allows either NYSE or NASDAQ to look for buyers.

NASDAQ began as a national association of dealers, but has evolved into a major world stock market. What makes it different from NYSE is that it is totally electronic-operated. NASDAQ utilizes NASDAQ 100 (NYSE utilize Dow Jones Industrial Average) as the stock market index to serve as a benchmark for the whole market. NASDAQ 100 comprises of 100 of the largest companies in terms of market value that trade their shares in NASDAQ. A company may be removed or added to NASDAQ 100 depending on their value ranking.

Usually, NASDAQ and NYSE are listed side by side on financial channels or across the news. These two exchanges differ in their time of trading. Though both normally operate from 9:30 a.m. to 4:00 p.m. on weekdays, the NASDAQ has a pre-market and post-market operation that allows trading outside the normal trading sessions. The pre-market session starts at 7:00 a.m. and ends at 9:30 a.m. while a post-market session occurs between 4:00 p.m. and 8:00 p.m. EST.

CHAPTER 2 – WHAT ABOUT NASDAQ AND NYSE?

Introduction to NASDAQ

NASDAQ is an acronym for National Association of Securities Dealers and Automated Quotations. It is an online trading system. It is in this association where the quotes of stocks in the stock market are sent to the dealers in an automated process. Through this, the dealers can, therefore, make use of these real-time quotes to make buy or sell decisions. In contrast to the New York Stock Exchange (NYSE), there is no physical trading that happens in the exchange center. This manner of trading thereby eliminates the need for jobbers and other market makers since dealers can trade directly through a web interface.

NASDAQ is considered the largest trading system in the world in terms of the number of daily trades exchanged after acquiring the American Stock Exchange. Because NASDAQ has more technology stocks than any other exchange, it has become popular among the traders. NASDAQ, too, has its own indices and the most popular are the NASDAQ 100 and NASDAQ Q. Other indices competing with NASDAQ are S&P 500 and DOW Jones as they represent many companies within the United States.

Before a company can be listed on NASDAQ, they need to follow a set of rules and regulations required by the association.

When you are learning about NASDAQ, you must also take note of its indicators - NASDAQ100, is the pre-market indicator, while NASDAQ100 is the after-hours indicator.

The pre-market indicator is calculated by using the last trading prices of the security between 8 a.m. and 8:30 a.m. EST. The after-hours indicator, on the other hand, refers to trades between 4 p.m. - 6:30 p.m. EST. Beginners may not find any significance in these indicators, but old time traders utilize this information in their decision-making.

Regardless of the kind of exchange you are dealing, you must analyze stocks before making a trade. Nowadays, massive information is being provided on every public trade stocks. However, these facts need to be weighed as you can be wrong in your perception.

Analyzing stocks can be complicated that you can easily get lost in the process. There are 12 basic steps that are used in analyzing stocks which are referred to as the NASDAQ Dozen.

In using this concept, you have to keep in mind that every stock has its pros and cons. By weighing these pros and cons, you will identify the best stock and place your trade on it. Here are the factors that are considered when analyzing your stocks.

- EPS or Earnings per Share
- ROE or Return on Equity
- Forecast Recommendations
- Earnings Surprises
- Days to Cover
- Insider Trading
- Weighted Alpha

- PEG Ratio
- Earnings Growth

Weigh your stocks based on these factors. Each stock must receive either a passing or failing grade.

Similarities and Differences in NASDAQ AND NYSE

Apart from the pre-market and post-market operation of NASDAQ, here is a comparison of these two trading organizations.

- The NASDAQ and NYSE are considered the two largest stock exchanges in the world. Both are located in the New York City. NASDAQ is known for its large selection of technology stocks which include Google, Apple, and Dell, among others. The NYSE has a larger cap than NASDAQ.
- NYSE uses human specialists in trading activity while NASDAQ operates on full automation.
- NASDAQ operates as a dealers market while NYSE is an auction market.
- For a company to be listed in NASDAQ, it needs to submit an application and comply with the following requirements
  - Must have at least 1,250,000 public shares with a regular bid price of $4.
  - Must be able to comply with the standards set by the government.
  - Must have at least $11 million aggregate pre-tax earnings in the past 3 years, $2.2 million in 2 years, and no net loss in a year, OR must have at least $27.5 million for the past 3 years, with a market capitalization over the last 12 months of at least $850 million and revenues of at least $90 million over the last year.

- To be listed in NYSE, an organization needs to submit a request accompanied with the following:
  - Articles of Incorporation and By-Laws
  - Annual Shareholders Report for 5 years
  - Copies of Stocks and Bonds Certificates
  - Form 10-K for the current year
  - Proposed Schedule of Expected Stock /distribution
  - Proxy statement derived from the present year's annual shareholder's meeting

The Organization is further expected to comply with the following requirements:

- Must issue a minimum of $1.1 million shares to at least 400 shareholders.
- Minimum market value of public shares must be $40 million at a minimum price of $4.
- Must have aggregate pre-tax earnings of $10 million for over the last 3 fiscal years, including $2 million in the most recent year. Another option to be listed in NYSE is based on a minimum global capitalization of $500 million, with revenues of at least $100 million for last year with no negative cash flow in the 3 years prior to application. A company may also be listed if it has revenues of at least $75 million in the last fiscal year.
- Over 1,860 companies were listed on NYSE with a market cap of $16.6 trillion in 2014. The NASDAQ list has a market cap of over $8.5 trillion with over 2,900 companies on the same year.

Trading in NASDAQ

Running through an automated web platform mechanism, NASDAQ is where buyers and sellers negotiate their business. The NYSE works in a double auction system where the highest bidder competes with other buyers and the lowest seller against other sellers.

The auction method doesn't work for NASDAQ. It is like a series of dealers selling stocks and maintaining cash and inventory. NASDAQ operates on web interface integration so you are instantly connected to dealers of shares available for sale.

There are two types of orders to choose from: the market order and the limit order. If you have a limit order, it means you are putting a limit on the price of the stocks you are going to purchase. Market order, on the other hand, is free and open. So regardless of the price of the current stock inventory, you are going ahead with the purchase.

What happens when the dealer has only 500 shares and you are placing an order for 1000 shares at market price? To fulfill this order, the dealer will provide you with the 500 available shares and the remaining 500 shares will be provided by another source. The price of which is dependent on the seller. It could be lower or higher. Now you can see that NASDAQ acts as an interdealer represented by securities dealers called market makers. These dealers are likely to compete with each other. Any person without trading experience can also have access to these bid offers. Overall,

NASDAQ is favorable for small traders and investors in the stock trading arena.

Trading in NYSE

NYSE is known as the biggest stock exchange in the world. Unlike NASDAQ which operates virtually, the NYSE operates in a physical location. All trading transactions here occur on a trading floor where traders openly display various emotions connected to their business actions. You can see traders waving their hand high, shouting at the top of their voices, or shaking hands in introduction or completion of a deal. NYSE is responsible for creating a sophisticated stock market that connects buyers and sellers in one place.

There are two types of stock markets. The **_primary market_** is where assets are deposited for trading to guarantee repayment. The **_secondary market_** is the place where traders are trading with the assets deposited in the primary market without the presence of the company issuing the assets for trading. The company is not directly involved in the trading but traded through a third party representative. A secondary market is a very common stock market and NYSE is the most esteemed secondary market in the world.

Companies like McDonalds, General Electric, and Gillette are just some of the large companies that prefer trading their stocks through a secondary market. In this type of market, a physical location is preferred. Brokerage firms are members of exchanges. Orders from companies are coursed through brokerage firms and are placed on the trading floor. There are people who are experts in linking buyers and sellers. However, prices of stocks are determined through auctions in a secondary market.

In an auction method, buyers expect to purchase the stock at the lowest price, whereas the seller is hoping for the opposite. When a trade is complete, the brokerage firm receives all the information pertaining to this particular trade and identifies the stockholder or depositor of the securities. In this process, computers are utilized and shareholders can launch an order electronically on the trading floor. Aside from NYSE, we have two more stock exchanges in the United States, the NASDAQ and AMEX. The NASDAQ has become a tough competitor for NYSE. Shares of stocks of large companies like Microsoft, Dell, Intel and Oracle are being traded by NASDAQ.

CHAPTER 3 – LEARNING TECHNIQUES FOR SUCCESSFUL TRADING

Avoiding Trading Mistakes

Trading is a risky and challenging endeavor for any novice. For years, traditional trading was an almost impossible pursuit for the inexperienced. Today, with easy access to the internet and integrated web interface, you can easily get into day trading. If you can withstand day trading in spite of the risks and costs, you need to familiarize yourself with the common mistakes that have ended the careers of many traders.

Impatience to wait for the right trade

As you are starting to get into the trade, exhibit the patience required in waiting for the right trade to match what is needed in your trading plan. Timing is crucial in buying or selling stocks. Never commit mistakes by forcing a trade, entering the wrong price, or overtrading your account.

Not setting up a set of rules before starting a trade.

There are two things that successful traders choose to do when they start trading. One is focus on trading, and two, think about the rules. You cannot do both of these things at the same time. You need to stay objective and rule out your emotions. The fear of loss will lead you to make a wrong decision. This is why it is important to start your day by setting up your entry point, limits, and point of exit.

Getting carried away by the fundamentals.

Those who are new in trading buy stocks based on a company's reputation in the business, forgetting that fundamentals don't matter in day trading. Traders must follow market signs instead of worrying over the fundamentals of the company they're trading. Buy stocks because of the benefit of the price and not because of the value of the company that traded it.

Averaging down.

Averaging down means buying more stocks when the price goes down believing it will recover soon. Because of the length of time involved, this kind of technique never works for day trading. You, therefore, need to set a limit on your losses and know when to let go of your position.

Indecisive as to when to get your profits.

The decision of when to get a profit is hard for a beginner. It's either you are holding your position too long or releasing it early for fear of missing a profit. Remember again that you either focus on the trade or remember the rule. When you get out of your position within minutes or seconds, you won't have enough time to do either of these.

Leaving your computer while you are in a position.

Experienced traders never leave their computer when they are in a position. A minute or 2 away from it can mean a loss, as a price change that will affect their position can occur in seconds. Never leave your position while it is open.

CHAPTER 4 – STOCK TRADING SOFTWARES

Do Trading Systems Really Work?

In today's trading system, you need a powerful trading tool or software that can really work. It is crucial for you to make a selection among the many automation tools being offered in the market today.

How to Choose the Best System for Day Trading?

To avoid getting confused in choosing what's best for you, here are some things you to consider in your selection.

First – Find out what the software targets. Is it aiming for specific target markets such as penny market or general stock market? You must be aware of the pros and cons of both markets. You must choose which one is suited to your personality, behavior or character.

Second – Can this tool provide you with the right calculation, analysis, and filter the best pick of stocks with the greatest potential for earning? Can it provide you with alerts and notifications regarding its choices? It is quite difficult for a normal trader to keep track of the stock market scope manually. The tool that can process all these data and provide you with the needed summary application would be perfectly right in your trade.

Third – Consider the consistency of the software. Is it stable in its performance? Know the winning rate of the software. You can do this by examining the records and testimonials provided by the product designer or creator.

Lastly, the most important point, is the guarantee for money back. This will not only guarantee you against fraud but it also signifies confidence and trust of the creator in the product he created. It is to your advantage if you can have a hands-on experience with the software before buying it.

CHAPTER 5 – IDENTIFYING PITFALLS IN TRADING

Advantages and Disadvantages

Advantages

- You can set your own hours
- You don't have any boss other than yourself
- You can work wherever you are and whenever you like
- You can gain financial freedom

Disadvantages

- Trading can be stressful
- You had to master self-discipline and patience before you can gain from the trade
- There is no security in your finances
- You can lose money anytime
- You spend long hours learning before you can earn

Risks in Day Trading and How to Avoid Pitfalls

The prospect of earning big through day trading is what has driven more people to go into trading stocks. They have gone about learning more of the trade trends, flows, and movements. If you are one of these people who have developed an interest in the trade industry, before you rush out and start investing your money, don't fail to consider the fact that there is always another side to a story. There are pitfalls in this industry that you need to avoid if you don't want to fall down as fast as you get in.

A common pitfall for a beginner is making a trade without understanding the market and strategies involved. This can eventually lead to money lost. Another common pitfall is making a fast pile of money without understanding the movements of the market so you can make a wise investment both at the present and in the future. Never invest money in the stock trade when you can't afford losing it.

Losing money is a part of trading. When you lose some, it doesn't mean that it's time for you to give up on trading. Remember that the stock market is constantly on the move and there are always chances losing in the stock market. Even expert traders are still losing money. The key here is to end up making more money in the long run, than what you have lost along the way.

Be sure that you are keeping track of all your trading activities, so you will know if you are losing or winning.

Keeping track of your investments is essential to find out what your bottom line is.

Since there is no way for you to eliminate all the risks involved in trading, you might as well learn to minimize their effects on your investment. Knowledge can be your main tool for avoiding these risks before they can catch you off-handed. Take time to learn from other people's mistakes so you won't end up making the same mistakes!

CHAPTER 6 – ESSENTIAL TIPS

Basic Tips for Success

Dreaming of becoming a successful investor at day trading? Of the total number of people who have gone into trading, only a few manage to end up successful. Nevertheless, this idea is not impossible if you are serious enough with the trade and you know by heart the right resources and devices needed in day trading.

As I stated at the start, information and "tips" are highly regarded in this business as they prove to be the core of the game.

Tip #1 – Develop a Strategy

Planning is crucial to day trading. You can't just jump into trading without formulating a plan to guide you through the course. Never use your gut feeling or hunch in decision making.

An existing trade plan based on relevant information you have gathered helps you cut your losses and sustain the trade. Without a plan, you are sure to accumulate losses. Before you start, be sure to arm yourself with an effective plan derived from other successful stock traders.

Tip # 2 – Information is Essential

Never get into the industry without understanding what you're getting into. Others make the mistake of getting into the trade after hearing of other's success. There are some people who are luckier than others but luck alone won't make you successful. You may get a few days' success but that won't last for long. Remember that day trading is a business and not a game of chance.

Tip #3 - Arm Yourself with a Lot of Information

You can do this through research and understanding how the industry works. This alone can give you an edge over others who jump into the industry less prepared. The more you research about the trade, the more experienced you can be. Experience in this industry is gauged through the knowledge you have gathered and not by years in the business. Though of course, if you're just sensible enough, you will surely gain knowledge through those years.

Tip #4 - Avoid Overtrading in Stock Exchange Websites

Never try to guess unpredictable market movement, especially when you are still new in the industry. Just get in a trade when you detect a red alert signal based on your plan. Overtrading can reverse your hard earned profits and bring your trading choices to their worst.

Be sure to invest only what you can afford to lose. This means not going beyond your capital in each trade. The key to success is guarding your capital investment against losses. If you lose your capital, that will be the end of your trading career.

Tip #5 - Explore the Trade with Other Traders

Learning from the experiences of others is the fastest way to success. If you pick up ideas and lessons from their errors and successes and integrate them into your work plan and you will find yourself learning through the process.

It is essential to establish relationships with fellow traders. You can join online communities and participate in forums. You can read blogs, attend seminars and take notes on the pointers from successful stock investors. You will learn a lot from other traders. Try to discover the best strategy and use it until you master the trade.

Use these tips in your day trading and other investments as well. Trading can be made profitable if you make the right decision and are given the right tools and devices.

No one can tell you exactly how much you can gain from investing in day trading but you can increase your earnings once you learn more of the trade and have a steady strategy to use.

A Step-by-Step Plan Guide to Trading Success

Formulate a Business Plan

As day trading is a business endeavor, you can develop a high probability rate of success if you are initially equipped with a business plan that includes the following:

- List of equipment, like a high-speed computer with an internet connection. Also, invest in a backup for emergencies.
- List of learning resources about day trading that can back you up in your endeavor. You may start on a course that will teach you about predicting market movements and trends.
- A projection of minimum profitability based in whatever course of action you will take.
- A budget requirement that includes expenses associated with your business.

Design your Own Trading Plan

There are many trading philosophies and strategies. Experiment with them and decide what works best for you and stick to it once you start day trading. Identify your performance metrics. Can you determine whether or not you're trading successfully?

In creating your trading plan, try to answer or identify the following:

- Try to define your trading edge.
- Know the kind of signals that will indicate an opportunity for a great trade.
- Identify the kind of stocks you want to trade. Are you interested in trading only those under a specific price target?
- Are you watching for subtle movements in heavily traded stocks?
- Prepare an exit strategy. Know when to close out a position in the market.

Be Ready for Losses

Losses are a normal part of trading. Successful traders boast of great losses before they mastered the art of trading. It's those failures that give you lessons on success. Just be sure to pay close attention to situations that are actually blessings in disguise. Don't waste time crying over your losses but learn from them.

Prepare for the Unexpected

Playing the stock market is full of risks. It's like being in a drag race where there are wild movements, unforeseen dips, and even inexplicable turns in the movement of prices and in almost every aspect of trading.

Practice Makes Perfect

Before plunging right into trading, try practicing daily before doing it in real time. Because of modern technology, this is possible through TD Ameritrade. With their web interface, you are allowed to trade without using real money. It is absolutely risk-free. You can set up an account and pretend you're trading real stocks. Go, set up your account and practice daily. This will give you a real hands-on training in day trading.

Trade to Win!

It's easy to go with your emotions when fear of loss takes a grip on you. You can easily succumb to an impulse to sell your stocks when you think you're about to lose. Before you turn your back, remember how much time and effort you have invested into crafting a trading strategy that is capable of bringing your success in the future. Just hold on to that strategy and keep your emotions out of the process.

Avoid changing strategy when you think it's not working anymore. Never change your strategy just because you're losing money. Change it only for a better one when there is a fluctuation in market dynamics, such as market instability.

Keep Abreast with the Current News

It's important to keep abreast of the current news in order to understand the current market situation. You can review financial news related to stocks. Some news is embedded in your trading platform. Check also on websites that provide news on stock trading like CNBC.com or TheStreet.com for news updates on stocks.

Keep a Journal

Keep track of your daily trading activities to review and analyze your performance for the day. Determine the success or failure of each day and what caused them. Did you incur a loss because you did not stick to your strategy? Log this information in your journal for future reference.

Learn to Adapt to Ever Changing Markets

You can't fully figure out the stock market. It is constantly changing and evolving. It is basic that you must stick to your trading strategy just because you're losing. However, you must also be perceptive of market movement. This is primarily what the stock market is all about. It works on perception.

You need to adapt to the market as it changes. Getting apart from it means losses for you. Change your strategy based on underlying changes in the markets and not because of emotions or fear of loss. Increases in market instability is a good reason to adapt to the market change.

Stop Hoping for the Best when Things are not Right

When you notice that a trade you're working on is no longer working according to your plan, don't waste time hoping things will change soon. Hope is never a sound trading technique. Make the appropriate call when you are in a losing position. Don't forget to stick to your strategic plan in times like this.

Place a Stop-Loss with Every Order

A stop-loss provides a graceful exit out of a losing position. This is the best way to avoid a great loss on a bad trade.

Use Limit Orders

Putting a price ceiling on your order is a wise decision as the market price can instantly swing at any moment.

Never Chase Stocks

When you stumble upon a great stock which you believe can earn you a great profit, start bidding. When the bid price rises up, you chase it by increasing your bid every time. This kind of activity must be avoided at all cost. Your aim in trading is to purchase stocks at a low price so you can sell it at a high price at the right moment. This is where discipline and control must come in.

Trading Secrets for Beginners

Day trading refers to the market positions which are held by traders only for a short time. As the name implies, traders typically buy and sell stocks within the same day. Many beginners make the mistake of treating day trade as a gamble – that is leaping into the bandwagon without applying tested stock trading strategies. They invest, not for the sake of business, but thinking they can get rich overnight.

Today, day trading is getting less complicated. Thanks to the modern technology which has made trading less strenuous and stressful than it was before. Once you learn a simple, rule-based trading strategy for anticipating market moves, you will realize it's not impossible to realize your goal. Here are some tips that will guide you in minimizing losses while you are still learning.

Secret #1 - Look for conditions where supply and demand are drastically imbalanced and make these your entry points.

A market is all about the law of supply and demand. When there is too much supply and less demand, the price is low. When there is insufficient supply and higher demand, the price is sure to rise.

Secret #2 – Always Set Price Targets

If you intend to buy a long position, make sure to decide in advance how much profit is acceptable. Also, set a stop-loss level to automatically limit your potential loss when the market trade turns against you. However, there is an exemption to this rule: If the market is strong, it is acceptable to set a new profit goal and stop-loss level once you have attained your initial target.

Secret #3 - Understand the proper risk-reward ratio.

As a beginner insist on a risk-reward of at least 3:1 when setting your targets. This allows you to lose small and win big. You can even come out ahead if you have a few losses in your trades. When you gain enough experience, then you can raise it up to 5:1 or even higher.

Secret #4 – Patience has its Value

It could be amusing to know that successful traders don't trade every day. They may be watching over the market movement but if they could not see any opportunity that meets their criteria, they remain inactive but watchful. Beginners often find it difficult to watch and not act, even when the action is not worthy enough.

Secret #5 – Discipline is a Must!

Again, stick to your strategic trading plan unless there is radical instability in the market movement. Other than that, don't deviate from your plan even if you're losing! Never expect to raise a fortune on a single trade.

Conclusion

Now that you have finished reading this eBook, I hope that you had learned the basics of day trading and you are now ready to start your first trade. Remember that knowledge is the first investment that you have to take and reading this eBook gives you the real edge over other beginners in the trade industry.

However, make learning a continuing process as you get deeper into day trading. Following all the tips provided here will help you as you go along the way toward success.

Good luck on your new endeavor and thank you for downloading this eBook!

www.ingramcontent.com/pod-product-compliance
Lightning Source LLC
Chambersburg PA
CBHW040815200526
45159CB00024B/2978